ALL BLACK EVERYTHING

⊣ ⊢

WESTON CUTTER

ALL BLACK EVERYTHING

WESTON CUTTER

NEW MICHIGAN PRESS
TUCSON, ARIZONA

NEW MICHIGAN PRESS
DEPT OF ENGLISH, P. O. BOX 210067
UNIVERSITY OF ARIZONA
TUCSON, AZ 85721-0067

<http://newmichiganpress.com/nmp>

Orders and queries to nmp@thediagram.com.

Copyright © 2012 by Weston Cutter.
All rights reserved.

ISBN 978-1-934832-34-9. FIRST PRINTING.

Printed in the United States of America.

Design by Ander Monson.

Cover image, "Tewksbury Hollow No. 10," 19" x 13" acrylic on panel, by Michael Wille.

TABLE / CONTENTS

No Parable	1
The Horse of St. Recall	2
Rural Causality	5
Clockwatcher's Halloween	7
is is light	8
How To Be Ready For Everything	12
Little Pink Houses	13
Real Maps to Chicago and Elsewhere	15
welcome to the game	16
so there	19
I Want You	20
Fareway Metaphysics	22
I used to think everything was part of a larger conversation	24

29	Rename the Birds
31	The Invention of Color vs. the Song of EA
32	Reveal
33	The Bodies of Atlanta
35	Minnehaha Creek
36	says who
38	Clothesline as Weather Forecast
40	‖‖‖‖‖‖‖
42	Mississippi

44	Rural Causality
46	Pumpernickel
48	When Ellen Is Gone
50	Lovesongs for Boxwrenches
52	No Science
53	Put the Sun Behind the Clouds
54	Lucinda Williams vs. Weinerdogs
57	*Acknowledgments*

This book is for Ellen.

NO PARABLE

Goodbye to the celery stalk days of our winter, the bare
cupboards, I want to believe again, breathe in the yellow
too much that is spring. February teaches patience like
a highway made entirely of snow, of unlit candles. I last
knew what to want when the days answered to October
and a thin coat was the easiest yes to shrug into place.
What comes red first are barns, the season receding like
an accepted apology, the wet metaphor that is Easter.
In the house I just left the dog still sniffs beneath the
cutting board, hoping for more to fall. To have fallen.
I too have spent my share of faith + the cherry picker
trucks off the highway's exit stand outstretched: we
reach, craft machinery for the same methods. When
it snows again—one last time before spring's taken
its seat at the table—I'll dream engines overwhelmed
by the river of my youth that floods each April, one
which answers no questions despite its whisper and flow.

THE HORSE OF SAINT RECALL

No mysteries and Lord the moon's
                               right where
           You last night left it
minus two, three degrees, today's heat

kicked my shins while the neighbor
                               -hood kids
           chased puppywild +
unschoolable through sprinklers,

dripping wet they took to the side
                               -walk in front
           of my house + never
glanced at the empty seat I'd set myself in,

Lord these late stages would be easier
                               to suffer prune
           and Metamucilly through
had the thunder struck when I was still

capable of lightning, tho electricity
                               maps our
           bones, and if You'll
never offer resolution on whether light

is particle or wave, from this canvas
                                  seat know
        I too Lord can be
duplicitous, can remember down

through tendons + the halflife of hemo-
                                  globin : I re-
         member both the minute
first spent kissing E's soft cheek and

telling myself *remember this, this kiss, skin*
                                  on lips. As if
        I'd ever forget either. Could.
Lord were I still streaky + soaked I too

would ignore empty men on empty
                                  porch chairs
        but Lord I'm not, and
Lord tonight I know the moon will be

right where you last night left it minus
                                  another few
        degrees : they're dim
arithmetic morsels you allow yet how

filling, Lord, how fulfilling, the just-
                              enough bit
                 none of us (in Your
   light, image, both) ever chew fully through.

RURAL CAUSALITY

I was in the basement among
colored piles, was where
I'd told my friends to go down and get high instead of risking
my neighbors hating   from day one
their new neighbor for hosting pot smokers on his front porch,
was in the room in which I'd killed
the baby snake which'd slithered past
our house's foundation's security system which consists of
concrete and wet Iowa dirt.
I was downstairs
because upstairs was a balloon I'd unintentionally inflated
through not speaking because I'd forgotten
balloons inflate by more than just air. I was
soap-handed + stuffing
shirts into a rapidly-filling pool and hoping, wasn't listening
for wind or warning, wasn't
considering how I'd left the TV tuned to some program
which was telling my absence
about a murder it would be re-enacting
which was so gruesome I should
leave the room, I was
thinking *pockets*
and *receipts*, was casting among folds for pens
and potential stains I'd left like lessons for my future self.
The Rorschach of a Thursday, how god
in certain ruralities is what elsewhere

would be called weather: even without light
it's possible to see what one believes in, hence faith. I was
in the basement when the power blew
and from the dark upstairs came Ellen's voice, we
Marco Polo'ed to each other   therefore spice routes+discovery—
our hands met first then the rest of our bodies, the creation of a *we*
in the dark—
and how forgiveness is simpler if undertaken blindly. Downstairs
clothes sat wet and unspun and the power
resurged hours later, trees still shaking
with the last twitches of storm, and
the lights which'd blinked
switchlessly off earlier reblazed sudden, appearing
throughout the dark house like a burning god
trying to tell us something.

CLOCKWATCHER'S HALLOWEEN

I don't ghost
or walk home shady anymore, I've dropped
all my form-

fuzzing coats
on old floors, have left them for other fears
to come shoulder

into shape.
I don't flaunt how I've given up on smoke,
the way my lips

now handle *hello*
when in I walk, my arms and bones nothing
more than what

to swing as ev-
idence of motion. Come here, evidence. Come
closer, ghosts. This

is how we move
now, the ways we dance. This is what we wear
to reveal it all.

IS IS LIGHT

What the problem is   is light : we're bare
  -ly outside, the dog tucked farther
into night : we're standing right
where people stand when   they step
 out side just for a minute : to let
 the dog   find some dark to sniff
   before more dreams of running : to
get   away from the selves and others
  the night offered inside : such crush : to
let our lungs   wrack icicle air between   gasps
     of heat : we're standing
   where we're   neither part   of dark
nor house's light : she told me earlier :
 when drinks were fresher : cooler : ice
 as yet unmelted : *you look like   you don't
 know how to belong   either* : what the prob-
lem is   is pupils, the body's   machinery
for receiving bright : how we're in the back-
doorlight's circumference while the dog sniffs
farther dark afield : how we're sneakouts : *how
about some fresh air* : how the dog   supposedly
needn't be tied up : *he   stays close* : so we've
been told : I can be seventeen when
-ever I need : can recall   a different night : forest-
thick, --deep-dark : a different girl ready to strike
a match : saying *close one eye* while she lit

what she then breathed : after the quick burst + first
  breath : after the extinguish : how she
  asked *can you still see fire with one eye?* : as if
I ever wouldn't again :what the problem is
  is   what we've all already   said : breathed :
  we live :[or learn to]: with the highway litter
of our utterances : we're things   pursued, car
  -toons : dust trailing our getaways : the
chasing cop of our vows obscured by
the dust of our momentum: we're out here
        : together : someone else's
  wife and whose   am I : we breathe fire
we   swear we've given up but still feel : we
cough now because conflagration's only
so hospitable : then the   dog's bark, maybe
  blocks off : and what is fire but a final
test : results of proximity : the hated hat
  and loved sweater curl up in flame   to-
gether : the forgotten   picture along with
  the slaved-over recipe box square   away
into ash : it's not even *our* dog   but now :
                now : now
there's this *us* out here : the far-off barks
getting   more distant : gaining darker slash
  farther ground : she closes eyes   and/or
bats lashes : she's somewhere   I'm not, right

next to me : *five bucks says he comes right
back, bet he just wants to chase something* :   : what
 the problem is is negotiation : my *come back*
whistle for our friends' dog's return :   the dog's
   return as excuse to retreat from this
 half-lit neither-here-nor- edge : inside
 the ice isn't arguing with the scotch +
somewhere I could stand and not wonder
 if it's where I should be standing : or
with whom : or why : her smile's loose,
 half-lit, she's smoked + her thirst slackened :
who knows how long I've been in
this dark : there's more quiet : we're listening
 for something : barks : *think that's
the last we hear of him?* : and then a running : pawthumps :
 the sniffing god of floppyears and lifted leg
tears around the garage : unpursued : unclearly
after some thing : who finally knows what
 any thing chases : she's looking at me: I at the dog :
there's so little to ever say, even when what's
 been sought's found : and then she opens : mouth :
smoke instead of words trail out : I believe
 for a moment I could look close + find
what fire inside leads to this : instead a hand
toward me before resting : on the door : back
inside : dog there at my feet : something's
   passed : maybe something could've always
been said : and maybe : whatever other god

there is   (of shivering   branches,   of iced
   roads, of   grown hyacinth) :   let   our words
linger as long as possible before they fall
   in dust :   the   shadows   our passings make :

HOW TO BE READY FOR EVERYTHING

is
      to pick up yesterday + crack
its thick honey. How
to be ready is not pockets
      but matches, the act
is never *carry* but *burn* or if not burn at least warm, the rote mem-
      orization that is flame. How to be ready
for everything is to know
      leaves turn, offer
their silver undersides when rain's
      coming, that you must use
heat and hard soap to scrub all trace
      of gathered apples
from your hands if you don't want
      the dog jumping lickwild. How
to be ready for everything is to know
you've got one name though
      nobody knows what it is,
even you, and so there's treebranch
      and rocksalt, there's shaved ice
      and trampled grass, there's a season
whose secrets haven't been disclosed
but look at the sky, look what's on its way.

LITTLE PINK HOUSES

Now I don't cover as much sky. Now I live
    in the promise and actuality of a ring
of highway that wraps this city. Now this
    is still the Midwest but like cousins
lined up there's variance, the tiny shifts
    that make someone more or less
likely to end up worthless, confused, stuck
    on one of life's sideroads muttering
I didn't even know I was lost. Now I know that
    Indiana is not one long John Cougar
Mellencamp song though like most I can't
    help always keeping a look out for
the Platonic ideal of the little pink house. Now
    it's Sunday and friends from Chicago
are upstairs sleeping off their beer + transit
    + now I don't close my eyes and
see Chicago when I think of love. Now
    my love lives with me in this ring +
living with love means paint samples, delib
    erations where once there were only
quick trigger decisions + so now when I close
    my eyes and think of love I see
my wife on a ladder, roller in hand, the wall
    changing color at her touch. No one
ever tells you there will always be enough
    ways to get lost, or that getting lost

is, like leftovers, delicious if predictable. No one
> mentions it may not have even
been Chicago to begin with, as it may not
> have been Minneapolis or Madrid or
Virginia: no one wants to believe that the mythic
> *somewhere* of our lives could just
as easily have been *anywhere*. Now I live
> on ground that's the same and different
from ground I've lived on before: dig here,
> find clay instead of the lush loam
that's underfoot where I believe I'm from but
> down three spadefuls + the dark's
the same as any place I've ever known.

REAL MAPS TO CHICAGO AND ELSEWHERE

  Some mornings go slow   as   timber,
time stuck snowbound, an icicle   shook
 free in night's wind : from the vent, house's
 south side : a question I can't   stop whistling
through my broken/fixed teeth has to do
  with direction and its play : paths : routes :
call that   south, where the garden's best planted,
  where   we look into the darkness   that
  separates   our sick neighbor's   house from
  our own : he leans desperate on doorframes, can
make   it from the backdoor to   his car only
 with   a solid push and who knows? We know
 no   names, not his, what   he suffers from,
what   he chooses   to call us, his who knows
 nameless neighbors : or say north : the direction
I'd   for now claim to head if lost to get   where
what I've always called home may   or may not
still remain : some mornings   I know   how to
  get to Chicago, to get to eggs toast + coffee,
the route to   take to my love's love :   all
   mornings   I hear machines, engines propelling
who   knows what   who knows where : to home
in sickness : in darkness to   the word   for where
 we are : I close my eyes : listen for telltale clicks,
           hints that time   knows the way :

WELCOME TO THE GAME

Ellen's face is where my lips belong as between
                 the candlesticks is where
the salt and pepper belong.
                     Before this table

and kitchen, before us, these candlesticks had
                 a place in a cupboard but
that cupboard quit when
                     when my grandfather

returned to fire and Minneapolis quit being
                 where he belonged. So
goes everything: birds throw
                    themselves into

wind, flap furious, gain no ground, the algebra
                 of their days zero sum.
Welcome to the game.
                   And so math

is everywhere, meaning Mr. Brown was right
                 in 9th grade though most
of the past is not right.
                     For instance: Monsa,

the special ed kid who sat 2nd back on the bus's
             right side, how he daily
fought to ignore our brays +
             mimicking stutters,

to keep dead-eye focused on the plastic z in
             the window. That whole
year, the z bus, it's vinyl
             green backseats

where I tried to belong among stoners + early
             smokers, all us carrying
scent as badges,
             evidence: I smelled

like nervousness, they of various poisons, we
             all hoped at 7:25 to get
through another day punch
             -free. Still: *Baaaaaa*

we'd bleat spastic in passing, Monsa z-focused,
             and we believed—who
knows—we were more,
             better, stronger—

we were no different: Monsa and us pimple-
            pickers + goners, we all
swam dread + filed
            sullen off together

at the school's entrance because everyone belongs
            to cold, winter Minnesota
mornings. Say he be-
            longed inside any

-thing better, a bus not stuffed with truculent sons
            of bitches, say any letter
would've been better than
            that so final z. Half

a life later I tell myself I belong where beauty knows
            my name + kisses me for
no reason, where I can
            empty my head's salt-

shaker wherever I please, and when I look at Ellen
            I want to tongue my way
backward through every
            last alphabet.

SO THERE

32 and used to it + now looking
to discontinue the pennies of
my youth, the coppery bits
bright and promising as a gumball that loses
flavor after six chews, seven, the only
place we could even find
such gumballs was in the entrance
for Snyders which was where we went,
age 9, when we finally got around
to telling our parents about the project
due the next day on which, no, we hadn't
done any work + so late-night homework
+ mewing anxiety, the feral cat of the
oh shit fear we'd more fully understand
years later when taking calls from loves whispering
      I'm late
or the later nights of our ambery 20's,
driving home belly full + one eye closed
sucking pennies because we'd heard
the act would help if we were confronted
with a breathalyzer, to think we ever
believed any currency—pocketed, sucked,
sunk into a good-looking truck, dark red,
plunked into any pool, wish attached—
would be enough to buy our way
out from inside our own, only breaths.

I WANT YOU

The smallest draft + the door slams, our lives
                       are the cause of so much wind,
the effects of. This morning breakfast
                       was the result of a winged bird
which can't fly, therefore sustenance
                       as turbulence of idea, design vs.
actual use. Examples abound: these hands
                       through centuries have learned
to make their way to ancestry tools—hammer
                       vs. pen, key in one, doorknob in
the other. Maybe we're all only coasting
                       on fate's breath, maybe I've made
my way to this room because eons back
                       some rock fell on a Neanderthal
not related to me, which raises questions
                       of luck and kismet, questions re:
my failure to listen as my future wife
                       tells me of her day's drags,
and every time I don't listen I prove
                       the rock fell on the wrong neanderthal
and every time I don't listen invites
                       a turbulence of self, of who
I hoped I'd be by now. Yes, there were
                       plans, for whom are there not?
But then different tools and meals, therefore
                       the man I hoped to become

(age 16, stealing peeks at thumbed *Cosmos*,
                      discovering How To Please)
remains turbulent, a self: our lives are cups
                      we tip and sip from, set right, refill.
We are both the drinking and what's drunk,
                      together in the dark or miles apart,
and the wind outside so loud so loud so quiet.

FAREWAY METAPHYSICS

I walk into the grocery store because something's
empty, a clear-plastic drawer of chilled air or
my idea for how to pass Saturday night hours
in such rurality the pigs here don't even cry
on their way to slaughter knowing no one will hear,
I walk into the grocery store because outside
there's rain but inside are boxes of crackers, canisters
of concentrate, because here I stand before shelves
of cheese + imagine my stomach's satisfied mooing,
because here I'm confronted by the fact that
all I choose—produce or kisses, this dog park or
that loafer—hinges on notions of vividity, some
mystic arithmetic I can't articulate any better than
I can the shocking glory of the curve of my wife's
thigh, the wordlessness that overwhelms the moments
we fit together in storms or bedrooms or confusion
over whose plan for a weekend is best and
the old song croons, she says tomato and I say tomato,
but the trick's of course that emphasis is what
we attach (like graffiti, bumperstickers) through
experience—the smell of hair in the morning, how
any hunger's satisfied—so you say *Ellen* and I
say *Ellen* but what I mean is my heart, the river
my soul's lived next to wherever I've lived, a view
in every direction for miles of rolling, fertile land
electricity sometimes longs so deeply for it allows

itself to become lightning, just for a moment +
what you mean is you walk into grocery stores,
too, for your own reasons, sale-priced cocoa, for
pineapple you can imagine goldly glistening once
you remove, with largest, sharpest knife, its
protective skin + however any of us plan to solve
questions of emptiness we'll all eventually pass
a pyramid of red tomatoes from everywhere,
the world over, and before them some of us will mouth
the only name we know, both hunger and hunger's answer.

I USED TO THINK EVERYTHING WAS PART OF A LARGER CONVERSATION

but maybe there's only the boats
    susurrating to the buoys + shore. Look:
if you see boats in every direction
    you're either from where I know, a place
which kisses some lake too much
    to call anything other than great, or you're
hollow and hankering to be filled
    in. Along the bike path mornings after
storm the blown branches betray
    how thin the myth of connectivity re
mains despite facebookery + www.
    whatever.com yr even now telling yrself
u won't waste such hrs browsing.
    2morrow. We all want to be filled in, all
hope we're the choicest blank form
    yet devised. Let's find fire + stand honest
before it: at the Chinese diner where yes
    terday I ate lunch there waited by the door
a box marked *Lost and Founded*, in it
    the usual, hats counter-toply abandoned,
shirts left ghosting chair backs as
    owners bolted. A woman I once knew as well
as weather cried weeks because she
    was sorrowed by the lack of a thing the size
of a bean. Nothing's the same size

    as how we carry it deeper in, beneath what's
been lost and founded: I used
    to think I knew what drinks to order all
my friends, what stories to tell to tug
    them from the murk they occasionally sank
into, lately all I know is salt, how sweat
    can find a reservoir in any elbow, how tears
end wherever they've spent their viscosity.
    Let's build satisfied tongues with whatever's
been left here. Let's say what we can.

RENAME THE BIRDS

Once was joy I ran toward and from. This treelined
path. Dusk and sunrise, counted footfalls. Once
was wonder. Used to rename the birds at each
turn of the trail—finch was swooping yellowflash,
jay a darting bluething. Hopalong redbreast, petulant
unblinking squawker that waited till the last minute
to fly away. Home was a cup of coffee, a kiss I'd recognize
from a thousand paces. The intake of breath before
my own name was whispered. Miles became more miles,
hopalong redbreast became dirty rustbird,

then burnt-out candle, then just redbird. Same bends
in same road, same birds, same breath over immeasurable
footfalls I'd never stopped counting, sure I was after
a quantity, some tally. Convinced I'd recognize
the number once I found it. Redbird, yellowbird, then
just birds in the way. Home as place where quiet
was quietest. Then simply to run, wordless, no
naming anything. To say nothing of overhead branches
hanging too low, stupid other runners. Used to be joy,
wonder at the way rain clung to branches like even water

knew better than to let go. Birds cut across grayblue
of sky, curve of an old lover's hand. Can't rediscover
joy, have to reinvent it every time. Redbird returns as unlit
winged firecracker. Miles don't become more miles,

already are miles. Footsteps just that, no number, no tally. No *ah-hah* numeral. Home is wherever you're headed next. At best a direction. Rain stuck in clouds like a name in a heart and when the sky sparks electric it won't matter what I'm running from when the water comes for me.

THE INVENTION OF COLOR VS. THE SONG OF EA

Muddy my love, love, lick my face
with your black boots, shudder my heart's tick
with your own talking hands, explain
without words what you see when you see me
senseless + overawed, joint-achingly
jangled in a love made of nets made
of almost-but-not-quite-forgotten-melodies
made from the nectar of a fruit never
named or harvested or tasted, detail
with your fingers on my clockless arms
the dance-hall 2/4 call of your name, palm
your rhythm wherever you can feel my heart then
pound the song I know you know against
the drum of my want, trill your yesses and
orchestrate the sudden silencing of questions
and then it's quarter to eyes open, and then it's
half past kiss: in this composition the blue
that is the color of desire must be considered red.

REVEAL

This is the letting   go: how   the light
 slips   from the   room, arms from
a sweater.   Cast wide enough,   you'll
find your   real wound: the street, alive
   with   memory,   springstrewn: last
year's leaves, debris like   fragments
  of once-great   machinery. I left   this
 and   this along that street;   I keep
leaving. Dark and   two cars   pass,
 one red   overtaking another.   This
   is the only   view,   all that'll ever
                        be revealed.

THE BODIES OF ATLANTA

If a woman's removing a turkey from the oven
the commercial will be for erectile dysfunction pills
or a self-wringing mop and if my wife's wearing cut-off
jean shorts it's my dream of what 1989 would've been like
had I been born earlier than 1978 with a taste
for Budweiser summers and when two doors down
the piano starts up with chopsticks the kids have
found the far shore of how much practice they
can tolerate and have earned back their fingers
+ time signatures. Tonight will be September.
Tonight will be 67° and falling in Indiana. Tonight
will be the blue ping-pong of self when the house
lacks half its inhabitants + fingers aren't enough:
what's lovely in being able to pluck a chip from a bag,
a book from a shelf, if there's no shirt's buttons to
later undo, breath held? For dinner I'll eat bread
alone in the silence of none of the lights complaining
of not being lit. Tonight will be nothing
turned on, time signature indiscernible. Tonight
will be when I remember the story of the Russian bells
which rang for decades even after they'd been buried, all
the townspeople could hear them. In erectile dysfunction
commercials the candle's never shown being lit,
only as it's hintingly huffed as pill-enhanced passion
commences offscreen. Tonight my favorite answer to
the day's questions will fall asleep with her flesh

all to herself far off + if it's a candle I blow alonely
out or a lamp I click off the light will leave
the room the same either way, either way the room
too big + bed doubly so + the night'll cool like
an engine soundless in the stalled car dark.

MINNEHAHA CREEK

We were looking for something more powerful. Startle
    of starlight, sodium bulbs buzzing dim and steady
as a headache. And the stairs leading down, then down
    again: the old creek choked with, what—

same old pennies. And not even unfolded wishes. Late
    enough and in the wind the willow limbs touched
steady moving water like what, like words, like this:
    We were looking for something new

to sing along to, the water humming against the stream
    -bed's stones, against the path of rocks too unstable
to walk across but for one week, two out of the year. And
    what of those old matchbooks. The

scribbled notes we never meant to remember this long. Never
    meant to keep. We were walking toward where one
water fell upon another water, where grass turned to mud
    turned to the music of passing. How

little we can ever see, even with everything all nightlit,
    plain and laid out as a whisper. *Remind me*, we said,
put our hands beneath that water, feeling for movement. *Show*
    me again, we said, one silence into another.

SAYS WHO

I won't forget tho
he asked me to, how—
how we were fifteen, those
dreaming years, liberties
further even than any
beyond we had right to—
he worked his guitar all
day, I had oranges to peel +
smoke to roll, a Jimi
Hendrix bio I felt like
I needed to consume as
proof of something—
trying for who knew—
the selves I had available
at age 15, adolescence
as perpetual Halloween—
her name was Cara, he'd
been singing, had rhymed her
with hair, bare, fanfare,
extraordinaire—we ate
frozen pizza, made fires
because we wanted to only
speak in flame, peed
standing on the porch's edge
in full view of passing cars
because fuck it, we were

alone; and later, at an hour
we'd learn as adults to
shoulder through with gin or
worse or better, some company
stronger than each other, he held
the big black guitar
upside down and shook it,
tried to dump out what
-ever it (with)held, eyed
the empty soundhole and
finally said *says who*, a line
that didn't rhyme with any name
he'd been thinking, all the
words we knew for desire, *says
who* he said again + we learned
from that to sing ourselves
to sleep, that was how many
girls ago, how many *says who*s
we meant to say louder
than we inevitably did, do,
as if what's truest is mumbled
only to the collars we've worn
or tried our best to approach,
Cara's, yours, whoever's.

CLOTHESLINE AS WEATHER FORECAST

even if not for rain, beneath these trees
 always there'll be some thing dripping:
  I've washed+hung the candy-colored
bathroom rug and the word for the desire
to eat that which isn't food is *pica* : sunny,
50% chance: etc.: what's weird yet true
 is that everything is made of heat :
a match has as much heat as a snow
-flake lacks and in just this way my bath
-room now has one lack of rug: my guitar
is inside, being played by nonhands
 as I watch my rug drip in sunlight: it was
supposed to rain three days ago+without
rain we have : we are: pretend other
  than that everything's one part ex-
pectation/one part lint : that meaning's
the difference between the two: a neighbor
 put a sign on the mailboxes saying he'd received
someone's French book on birds + would this
  someone please pick it up: then another sign,
same thing: then another, angry: *come on, just
take your damn French bird book already* and
instead of making signs I wondered why he wasn't
  learning the French word for sparrow,
how the French tongue the whippoorwill's
trill : the world, my friend,   is the heat

that's there   and the heat that's not, like
the amputee who, his phantom fist clenched
for all nine years he'd been handless, watched
  his remaining hand in a mirror   open wide
+felt the missing fist's ungrasping : I live
where there's a word   for the craving
  to taste the uneatable   but no way to
live with that need : what's most amazing
is not, really, that a bird   might find my rug
   on the line to shit on, but that all the nonbirds
will shit so much nonshit on it : how   strangers
come together, road over land,   rain + thunder
  missing a town : I have only guesses.

||||||||

—I've no new river but plenty
    still to flow to :
through : I'll never not be the kid
    who sniffled next to
the radio as cheesy keening voices
    thickened with what
I believed was real feel : I'll never
    not be just like you :
I too built the edifices of my own
    shivery emotions
by singing along, pretending to feel
    until I finally felt :
"hold
    onto the night"
meant mystery to me in third grade :
    + decades pass : now
I've learned like you to let go : now
    my wife and I howl
inarticulate hurts in the car : a Friday
    night that's slipped
either of our grip : we're approaching
    a city that's no longer
home : a song we used to wake up
    singing along to :
driving to swimming lessons my dad
    would warble with

radio songs, words he remembered
    or didn't, I'd go
throw myself into chlorine, hearing
    only water's churn.
                        When later we
    forgive each other
it's nothing more than chorus, same
    song : this is how
we learn : who knows if we've even
    got the words right :

MISSISSIPPI

keep treading : back up the liferivers
                we are: say life begins
    the minute a stranger's number's
       thumbed to phone : *saved* : I now
own a washing machine + so no longer sit
       in Spin Cycle's blueglow waiting
   for beauty to wink in + whisper *let's
get dirty* : outside it's October : outside
  the Ash are dying because they're delicious
to a bug that can't help itself : outside a bar ages back
  a girl who'd told me her name a baseball
     game's worth of beers before slurred
her number + I saved her as *girl* + never called
   + here I am, never forgetting : say
life's a choice against an oblivion we've barely
                            got   language
for : say life begins *in it*, the oblivion
which rushes like a thief into the post-first-kiss
moments : that *I can taste it* aftermath once hunger's
  taken shape + flavor : I no longer wash
my whites separate, am resigned to undershirts going
  a vague gray, the color   of the way it feels to not
know what to do on a Tuesday after lunch. Outside
it's Saturday : outside the lilac we shoved
into the ground   in rain   in September buds
where the autumn sun's tricked it : guess it : life's

nothing more than a bending toward warmth : (how
ever brief : great men die : each day) : outside
  half the day's offered itself : snow's   a 40%
chance : outside   those fleet+brief moments of
clear hunger we eat : what's closest : trusting
   our tongues + lips :   that's it :

RURAL CAUSALITY

Because the neighbor's yard speaks dog barks
and ours rattly dead leaves. Because the other
neighbor's yard whispers *come to me* from
behind a FOR SALE sign. Because the truck
has learned to conjugate the verbs of rust and when
I don't know what to say to my wife I say :
And how deep must we dig before finding
                    a sweeter dirt than what's snug
on the surface? Because God's neither season
nor storm and where we live the elemental word
is *combine*, both noun and verb, a way to fill
days and empty fields. Because there must be
some way to learn what I'm supposed to say
when I don't know what to harvest + in autumn
this whole town murmurs dust and sunsets
are burlap wonders. Because for years I planned
what I'd say before I ever began to speak there-
fore the self as daily failed improv. Because
at its edges this town is fluent in corn while down
its sleepy streets one's to say *welp* before a glance
is shot skyward, scanning for portent. Because
winter's coming as a secret that'll start in the garage's
morning shadow, at the lake's hardening edge.
Because the grass beneath the leaves can't hear
the wind's *go to sleep now* lullaby. Because for every
thing there's an underneath. Because it's not *nothing*

we drive through and/or past on the way to
the next town even if the landscape's gray matches
how dull hunger feels. Because my wife some
-times speaks in her sleep. *Fungo. Butchery pathway. I've
got a whole pocketful.* The trick seems less
about understanding language as reading emergency,
to know whether the neighbor's dog's barking
at meaningless blowing leaves or someone approaching
finally with the axe I've feared since my first
scary movie. Because scary movies and carrying
fears like a nickname. Because at this street's
corner all summer the manicured lawn drawled
this is how it's done while the woman laid in her chair,
sunbathing a race against the inevitable sag + pallor.
Because even nothing's got plenty to say,
has been holding it's breath this whole time :

PUMPERNICKEL

Earth movers stand at rest beside mounds
    of earth, a hundred unsent
love letters, bonewhite moon ghosting
    above abandoned machinery +
desolated highway, and Dr. Max is on
    latenight AM radio talking about
training dogs, how it's arbitrary, language
is loose as topsoil, one could just as easily
    say *pumpernickel* in place of *lie down*,
in place of *come here*: makes no difference
    to the dog. I've been on the road
for a dozen hours, nearly a day, one long
    enactment of almost: a zero-sum game
of betweens. I'm in Kentucky, or still
    Illinois, or I'm three hours from one
coast but driving demands measurement
    with different string: a thousand miles
from one idea of home, several hundred
    from another. I'm half a tank of gas
        from just giving up,
        lying down among corn
            in moonlight
            and waiting for day.

Dr. Max is going on and on, says most things
 come down to repetition, cause
and effect, call and someone will—, seek
 and ye shall—, etcetera. Home's
a shirt you've loved to pieces, worn good
 holes in. The bulldozer at the hill's
rocky base means nothing if you know behind
 the rock the hill's heart's still wet,
that a small stream is its core, that face
 is one thing but what's inside is still
being made, riverfinger by riverfinger, like
 how since I was six years old
I've never been able to fold my hands—
 even over a steering wheel, 2am,
past a construction site, under a sky
 littered with more stars than there are
names—without an empty cup in my chest
 righting itself in longing
for some watery, incantatory *amen*.

WHEN ELLEN IS GONE

I forget I will die and the wind is whatever
                          I hear no matter
what I listen for, the windows stay shut even
if I open them, in the truck as I drive
the dog to the hills at town's edge I can't say
                my own name: my love's

the same silver as anyone's and what I feel
                        will gather dust just
like a family candlestick or barn's window-
sill, the yards we pass are coming green
slow, April again, tulips delicately pushing
                  through, teaching the latest

conjugation of *emerge*: when Ellen is gone
                      I'm all empty
shirt, a wineless glass held long past the last
sip. In the truck's bed the dog sticks his snout
out to read the newspaper air + supposedly
                  there once stood a rough-

hewn chapel among this hill's rolls. Imagine
                    the congregants,
knees on slivery wood, unelectric light if at
all. To stand in a doorway + look out over
the flat of one's life, who knows what they saw.
                In the hills the dog catches

scent, takes off, and I wonder what bone or
                            Rosary's trace he'll
run til he's found the source of. Such is love,
or what I've come to understand of de-
votion: when I whistle toward where the dog
                    disappeared the sound's

a smear, all gray, hints of perhaps blue +
                          what follows is
the sound of wind about to blow again.
The tree's bare branches, the sky a mumbled
answer about distance: when Ellen is gone
                I learn my life's truer prayer.

LOVESONGS FOR BOXWRENCHES

I built this mobile because I believe in
gravity but not Calder and I built these

lips because I wondered how you'd
taste after and I wrote all this music, these

lovesongs for box wrenches and ballads to
leafless trees and fugues for the confusion

of constant movement, just so I'd have
something to sing when it got too dark

to look you in the eye. I wrote all this yet
still god leaves, the earth slips the nets

we set each night. We wear our layers like
the leaves of autumn trees, whole rivers swim

within fish, the oceans pull moons from
my infinite body but my next song has

only the word *Goodbye* and it's incorrectly
whispered. I built these legs because

beauty is its own reason (though not
the reason for these legs) and I built this

house to hide in but I built this window
for you, for you to come see me. My next

song will begin soon enough with the last
words of the first Bible but until then

come sit at my window and pretend again
that god is lightning and thunder. If god

is not these fingers nor these guns nor
the squaredances people shake to ask

for rain, come sit with me and try not
to pray as the thunder finds its home.

NO SCIENCE

If you can't find yr way in, written on the edge of a brick :
it's August, heat and wetness thick as a scent
but I can find winter anywhere: the brick a member
of an old wall's army, remnants of cement : scabs : too
hot to sleep well : last night I lay down in my bed but
awoke in the next room's chair : and if the phrase is
complete in itself : *if you can't find yr way in* : perhaps
brick as answer : perhaps nothing : no answer : I'm
thinking *snow*, thinking my way arctic : relieving : the
brick's been sitting on a table I've passed dozens of
times, been sitting like a doomed prince, the kingdom
already fallen and him sitting in his last throne : all brick
walls just iterations of *until* : on the way home the long
walls of the church hold the summer day's heat : heat as
confession, brick as priest : private unto darkness : amen
: + at night, when it's cooler, 3pm August will still be
stuck in the wall, trapped : a name not quite forgotten
: spare heat for absent touches : *if you can't find yr way
in* and perhaps there is no way in : no *in* : how warmth
moves into brick : voices into dark : and before dawn,
day's bricks finally cool, their heat like secrets told to the
dark : ready again : again :

PUT THE SUN BEHIND THE CLOUDS

We offer each other old photographs: here's
                         me at this speed, that
latitude, before I said whatever I said that led
     here. This is how I looked before
I believed in possession, when all I belonged to
               was river, roadway, paths. We
use fingers, laughingly track unclicked shifts,
                         changes between
pictures: a disastrous haircut grown back out,
     there's a tattoo, nobody looks wasted
anymore, a different decade's garish style. We'll
              never wrap our hands around
all the red we each lived through in this room
                    where the sun's setting's
an orange shower. Here's you, seventeen: a new
     grin, face free, in your hand the glint
of your first ever keys. Tell me where you drove,
             what you sang as you got there:
tell me all the ways you've built the mouth that's
                  now my name's home.

LUCINDA WILLIAMS VS. WEINERDOGS

I've been circling: wandering around, looking
  for something bright : maybe chewable: to
-day the rain: enough to set the grass on fire
  with runoff: and the neighbor's weinerdog
had his first impression   of ocean: and   I
just walked through it: through worms: through
  old Lucinda Williams songs all day about seeing
something in someone's eyes: all day, songs
about almost-but-not-quite being alone: the coded
  what-if of a lovesong: an umbrella: the first
guy I walked past this afternoon, both us watching
the wetground in front of us, had an umbrella with
  words printed on the inside: *Sunny!* it said :
Clearing up! : my umbrella's black as a sixteen
year-old's wishes: as a lung: the man   and I
  did not   nod as we passed, and later, over
coffee, I told Carrie I'd been looking for something
bright all day and she asked if I'd ever heard that
Lucinda Williams grew up in the same town she
kept singing about, song after   song after : and
  if that wasn't enough circling,   looking for some-
thing bright there was, she said,   a place across
the street that baked cookies   every ten minutes
  all day long: and past that   an animal hospital :
then hills: memories of drives   I wanted to take
but didn't   because I couldn't figure out where

I wanted   to end up   and finally, eventually, if there's
enough gas in the light in the car in the sky   she
 leaned black, black coffee in a white mug in her
small hand, eventually, she said   there's   the ocean: the
sky's edge shaped   way out   by dull, blinking buoys.

ACKNOWLEDGMENTS

Thanks to the editors of each of the following, where some of these poems appeared earlier:

BOMBlog, Contrary, Crazyhorse, Cream City Review, Devil's Lake, DIAGRAM, Eleven Eleven, Jelly Roll, Kenyon Review, Laurel Review, The Literary Review, Lumberyard, Mid-American Review, Muzzle, Nashville Review, Ploughshares, Red Cedar Review, Salt Hill, Sixth Finch, Sugar House, Tusculum Review, West Branch, Willow Springs, Witness.

"I Want You" was republished on *Verse Daily*.

Massive thanks as well to Bob Hicok and Tom Gardner, to Jennifer Boyden and Olena Kalytiak Davis, and to Joel Brouwer, Jake Adam York, and Ander Monson.

COLOPHON

Text is set in a digital version of Jenson, designed by Robert Slimbach in 1996, and based on the work of punchcutter, printer, and publisher Nicolas Jenson.

WESTON CUTTER is 1) from Minnesota, 2) the author of the story collection *You'd Be a Stranger, Too* and the poetry chapbooks *Plus or Minus* and *(0,0)*, and 3) an Assistant Prof at the University of St Francis in Fort Wayne, IN.

NEW MICHIGAN PRESS, based in Tucson, Arizona, prints poetry and prose chapbooks, especially work that transcends traditional genre. Together with DIAGRAM, NMP sponsors a yearly chapbook competition.

DIAGRAM, a journal of text, art, and schematic, is published bimonthly at THEDIAGRAM.COM. Periodic print anthologies are available from the New Michigan Press at NEWMICHIGANPRESS.COM/NMP.

www.ingramcontent.com/pod-product-compliance
Lightning Source LLC
Chambersburg PA
CBHW031310060426
42444CB00033B/1160